In the Library of Lost Objects

Noel Duffy

Ward Wood Publishing
www.wardwoodpublishing.co.uk

Published by Ward Wood Publishing
6 The Drive
Golders Green
London NW11 9SR
www.wardwoodpublishing.co.uk

The right of Noel Duffy to be identified as author of
this work has been asserted by him in accordance with
the Copyright, Designs and Patent Act, 1988.
Copyright © 2011 Noel Duffy
ISBN: 978-0-9566602-8-2
British Library Cataloguing in Publication Data. A CIP
record for this book can be obtained from the British
Library.

Designed and typeset in Palatino Linotype by
Ward Wood Publishing.
Cover design by Mike Fortune-Wood.
Cover photograph by Gemma Mc Guigan, courtesy of
the artist.
Printed in Great Britain by the
MPG Books Group, Bodmin and King's Lynn

In memory of my father, Tim Duffy

Contents

Acknowledgements

These poems, or versions of them, have appeared in: *Poetry Ireland Review, Force 10, Electric Acorn* (online), *The Poetry Mill* (online), *Ropes, Limited Edition, The Cúirt Journal, Bellingham Review* (USA), *De Brakke Hond: Special Irish Issue* (Belgium) and *Carapace: Special Irish Issue* (South Africa), *Sunday Miscellany* (RTÉ Radio 1); and in the anthologies *Slow Time: 100 Poems to Take You There* (Marino Press, 2000) and *The Open Door Book of Poetry* (New Island, 2005) both edited by Niall MacMonagle, and *RTÉ Sunday Miscellany: a selection from 2008-2011* (New Island, 2011) edited by Clíodhna Ní Anluain.

'Daisy-Chain' was the winning poem in the Fingal Scribe Poetry Award, 1999.
'The Moons' was the runner-up poem in the Universe Poetry Competition (to mark the Einstein centenary) in 2005.
'His Hands' was shortlisted for the Bridport Prize in 2008.

A selection of ten poems from this collection was awarded the START Chapbook Prize and published as *The Silence After* (South Tipperary Arts Centre, 2003). Another selection won *The Firewords Poetry Award* (Galway City Council) in 2005.

In the Library of Lost Objects was shortlisted for the 2010 Patrick Kavanagh Poetry Prize for the best unpublished first collection by an Irish author, receiving a special commendation from the judge, Brian Lynch. Noel Duffy was also shortlisted for the Over the Edge New Writer of the Year Award, 2010.

I wish to offer my sincere thanks to Sheila Phelan, Louis de Paor, Michael Gorman and Theo Dorgan for their insightful comments on some of the pieces contained in this book. My gratitude also to Niall MacMonagle, Grace Wells, Paola Uberti, Greg O'Brien, Beth Phillips and Mark Carter for their moral support. A great debt is owed to my editor, Adele Ward, for her close reading of the manuscript and thoughtful suggestions on the poems, and to Shauna Busto Gilligan for proofing the manuscript. My thanks to Gemma Mc Guigan for the beautiful cover photograph and to Brian Walsh for bringing it to my attention. Sincere thanks also to Mike Fortune-Wood for the cover design and all the other work he does at Ward Wood Publishing.

In the Library
of Lost Objects

Apple

Red of course. The colour
of blood. Shining and smooth,
its form perfected and round.
An emblem of the human

mind, nestled up there
among the leaves innocent
of its fate, swaying
in a green dream about

to waken. Ripe and
waiting for the final
nudge, the soft slap
of the breeze, to fall

down to the ground
with a thud beside
the place he sits, to
start again the ancient act

of the naming of parts.

Daisy-Chain

Sometimes on Sundays we'd take
the old canal bank walk
from Broom Bridge to the Ashtown Cross,
my father picking daisies as we went

between questions of *How is school?*
and *Did you score any goals this week?*
my embarrassment at his interest
saying, *Fine* or *Only one this time.*

Often he would talk about the past,
of how his grandfather passed this spot
every day for nearly twenty years
as he drove the train from Castlebar

to Connolly Station, the canal water
his sign that he was nearly home,
until his early death in a red-brick
terraced house near Great Western Square,

my father saying, *I only knew him*
by a photograph the way you know my father
through me, as an image and likeness,
as a man about whom stories gather;

and all the while his fingers working
the stems, binding them together one
by one, a chain of flowers slowly forming
in his hands until joining first to last

the circle was complete and he'd
give it to me to throw into the canal waters.
And forgetting school and football,
we'd watch it floating on the surface,

bobbing slightly in our world of lost
connections, the frail wreath pulled
slowly downstream by the current, towards
the distant, steady thunder of the lock.

The Beekeeper to his Assistant

You must understand from the beginning
that the hive is a mind and one
you will not comprehend. Behind

the frantic to-ing and fro-ing of the bees
order prevails: the honeycomb from nothing
builds itself by geometry alone, cell by cell,

the Queen its centre and circumference.
Even the pollen-drunk dance of the messenger
returned from gardens heavy with blossoms

is a kind of mathematical waltz, calculating
in each step the sun's slow orbit through
the heavens. For all the talk of the nuptial flight

no one has ever seen it, though it must happen.
Once in early summer I did see the Queen hover
by the hive's entrance awaiting the drones.

And they came, hundreds of them, greedy
for her scent. I saw them disappear into the shade
of the meadow in her wake. That was all.

When they returned to the hive at dusk
exhausted and sticky from their work, their wings
were snapped and they were thrown to the earth.

Not even the Queen can evade the will of the bees.
Unknowingly she gives birth to her own successor
incubated in the brood and hidden from her.

Without a sign her servants descend on her
in a swarm and she is smothered – by violence
the honeycomb becomes her honeyed mausoleum.

Yet, despite these explanations, I have told you
nothing. And the beehive has its secrets.

I live for those moments in late evening
beneath the lilac blossoms when the bees
gather in a cloud about me, buzzing flecks

of light like Einstein's vision. It is a door
into the heart of summer where time
seems to slip away and is lived through.

Vintage
In memory of Marty Duffy

I

Flash Harry my dad called him in jest. His
younger brother following in their uncle's footsteps
and making good: a big house and his own garage,
a love of expensive whiskey and vintage cars,
standing in the kitchen with his trademark cigar,
sovereign rings and fur-lined coat. To me
he was the image of success, arriving Sundays
in a Jag or Merc, patting my head and bearing gifts.

No room, it seemed, was big enough to hold him.

II

It was a tradition, the Duffy clan visiting us
on the weekend of the Phoenix Park Grand Prix,
sandwiches packed, a flask of tea, coleslaw, potato salad:
the family reunion to the sound of roaring engines
burning up the narrow roads and hairpins
as we sat on our fold-up chairs or climbed barriers
for a better view.

I sat on my uncle's shoulders. The cars descended
on the corner in a cloud of smoke, the sharp smell
of petrol filling our lungs with the momentary thrill
of the corner pile-up then the slow take-away and
    acceleration
as they filed out of the bend vying for position
and screamed off between the trees into the distance.

Marty was in his element.

III

We had driven to some stately home
in Wexford or Waterford. There was a vintage rally,
the great and good gathered for the spectacle.
We found Marty standing by his new MG,
a proud father. He had worked on it for months
and now it slumbered shoulder to shoulder
with the other marvels, shining white
in the afternoon heat, perfectly returned
to its former glory...

If only I could make such a restoration.

The Summer I Mapped the World

The globe was left at the back of the class
gathering dust, the light bulb that lit it up
long since gone out. But still I liked to look at it,
the whole round earth mapped
like a football of oceans and continents,
all precisely placed, it said in my geography book,
according to their latitude and longitude.

I wondered though why its axis was fixed
at a peculiar angle, not straight up as I had imagined.
I assumed the teacher had put it together
wrong like so many other things. 'Duffy!' he bellowed
as he stalked among the desks pulling me
from my reverie, 'The verb, *éalaigh*,
when you're ready. In the past, present,
and future tenses.' I couldn't do it, or wouldn't,
spent most afternoons locked in the classroom
with that fearsome man repeating lines
endlessly on a page, waiting as the clock ticked
slowly on for the summer to come.

And when it did arrive finally, I undertook
my grand plan: an ordnance survey of
my neighbourhood and environs (I'd seen
that word on an old Michelin map in my da's car),
bounded to the north by the Navan Road,
and to the south by the railway tracks
that passed by the GAA pitch and kept us apart
from the 'bad eggs' across the way,
who sat on the hillside drinking cider
and throwing stones down at the trains
on their way to the station.

And so each morning I set out to map
the crosshatched network of lanes and streets,
pedalling non-stop as I counted each turn out loud
to avoid mistakes – *twenty-one, twenty-two,*
twenty-three, twenty-four – until Stasia Clarkin
or some other neighbour would break my concentration
saying, 'For heaven's sake child what are you doing?
You'll wear yourself out!' and I'd have to start again,
counting silently this time, and writing
my totals into my green notebook.

Then returning to the house exhausted at lunch,
I worked all afternoon on the checked page
of my copybook with a ruler, pencil, divider,
and a primitive notion of triangulation
I'd stumbled upon in a battered copy of *Reader's Digest*
I borrowed from Dr Brennan's surgery waiting room.

But like two jigsaw puzzles with their pieces
muddled, things didn't quite fit together:
roads ran into empty whiteness; others
crossed over into their neighbour's driveways –
the O'Briens and Lynches lost their gardens
to the Walshes, the Kennys ended up
on the butcher's counter.

No matter how much I tried to put it right, re-cycled
each street twice to make sure of my measurements,
some other road vanished into the border,
or ended up adrift and isolated as though
the people who lived there would never escape,
would never go to school or work or mass again,
would only have each other to call to
as they stood alone in page-white doorways.

So, like all map-makers, when the calculation
didn't fit I modified my charts by eye and instinct,
so that the laneway opposite Mrs Murray's sweetshop
came out beside McLoughlin's overrun garden,
the playing field with its graffiti-covered walls
big enough for the summer five-a-side tournament.

At last the roads locked into place, joined up
as they should across the barren spaces,
forming the warren of streets I was so familiar with:
their trees and lampposts and tar macadam driveways,
their people in the gardens watering flowers
or tinkering with cars and lawn mowers.

Then one day in late summer I reached
the Navan Road and decided to keep going,
pedalling fast this time without counting till
I reached the boundary wall of the Phoenix Park.
I waited there at the gate terrified. I'd heard about
those weirdos in school who sat on park benches
near the zoo pretending to read the paper,
or drawing pictures of giraffes and bears.

Finally finding the courage, I pushed my bike
through the swing-gate and saw, with shock,
the vast territory beyond: enormous fields edged
by trees whose names I didn't know; the pathways
that twisted through the woods with no houses
or streets to fix them by; no up or down, no left
or right; no address to post a letter to
except their place beneath the open sky…

And I felt something like defeat and freedom
all at once. I sat down beneath the shade
of an oak tree to take it in, and reflected there
for a long time on my future: how in the autumn
when I returned to school I'd have a new teacher,
and prayed he'd never heard my name mentioned.

The Hiding Place

We are in hiding from our lives
the curtains drawn on our room,
the light filtering in through a small crack
onto the world, like our hope
reaching out across the lawn to find the trees
still rooted in the ground, the gravel path
leading to the gate as it has always done.
The world in its proper place and we in ours
not disturbing it, warm and tired
beneath the heavy covers as the day starts
to the distant stutter of a car as it climbs the hill
then passes out of consciousness
into the silence of the morning.

Captives
after Michelangelo

His mind has become
impenetrable as stone
each thought a hammering
chisel blow burrowing

for the grain in memory.
And to hack and cleave
at the surface thus
might reveal Atlas

buried there, buckled
and straining under
the weight of himself;
or Matthew clutching

the Word of Christ
his face turned away
in anguish. Or to continue,
another face,

perhaps his own, half-
exposed to the air,
half-consumed by
the element of its creation;

and a hand, the muscles
tense and ready for movement
as soon as the eye
stops looking.

Fossil

In this stark church of glass cabinets
we have made an icon of it.
I open the display-case with hushed reverence
and take the thin crust in my hands.
Suddenly, I feel the certainty of its history.

It is a kind of Christ etched in silicate.
I follow with my thumb the crippled
symmetries, the perfect lines of its form,
read the braille of that ancient calamity
when the waters abandoned it.

Preserved in stone: the mouth, the anus,
the ambulacra – and eyes that seem
to look across ninety million years and say
Stand still for just one instant
and nature will exact a brutal facsimile.

The Bee King

Precocious, fearless, funny: he was
the kid on the street we wanted to be,
gathering around him as he placed
a row of jam-jars along the wall

and waited for the bees to come
to his calling. And they did come,
tumbled into the jars one by one
as he quickly screwed the lids back on,

the bees buzzing frantically
behind the glass and growing weaker.
Half-dead and earthbound,
he took them up with tweezers

and laid them out on the pavement.
They reminded me of dusty insects
I'd seen in glass cases
at the National History Museum,

except they were still moving,
their wings flecked with pollen
as they shifted uneasily in the breeze
and he pinned them to the tar macadam

with short needles.
He smiled down at his collection,
then glared at us as he sat
among the heavy blossoms.

We watched in silence, knowing
we should turn away but unable to.
I remember it clearly.
I must've been there:

glass-eyed, staring, half-dumb
and curious as his mother called to him
from the porch to come for his dinner
– and he ignoring her.

Wasp

Big-eyed and satisfied
the severed head
of a wasp feeding
on marmalade
no longer wasp
merely wasp-head
somehow outliving
its own death
as it gorges
the honeyed water
from the bowl with
no stomach to hold it
no wings to lift
its broken body
from the place
of final pleasure.

The Book Collector

1. First Edition

Strange that I authenticate a work
not by the brilliance of its content

but by the errors of the printer's hand
as a letter is lost or jumbled

in the groaning print works.
The flaw. The mistake. The error

of judgement and oversight;
the missed detail and botched

sentence that runs into the page gutter
like a thought that was never finished;

the missing apostrophe and comma.
All the things that went astray

in the process of passing the thing
from one hand to another.

2. In The Library of Lost Objects

The words settle on the page
for the first time, like insects

fixed on their pins in a dusty museum.
Never before seen in the world.

A new thing, an order of words captured
and reinstated from the day's flux and insistence,

a sleight-of-hand trick that holds the world back
for a heart-beat...

Holds. Holds...

*

And then they are passed out into the city,
scattered to the corners like ragged confetti,

stacked in market stalls beside postcards and love letters,
lined like foot soldiers in toppling bookcases;

the unwanted gift or capricious purchase,
discarded, misplaced, boxed up, forgotten,

used to keep the wind from the chimney,
shelved absently in the library of lost objects

waiting for us to find them.

3. Inscription

And this one does somehow. Dog-eared
from use, weathered, ossified, organic,

surviving the memory loss and detritus,
the grinding entropy and metamorphosis.

Nothing much to look at, water damaged,
it finds its way to me in this haphazard thrift shop

among the tattered paperbacks and half-price
cookery manuals, the remaindered

astrologies with their outdated prognostications,
the promises of love that never happened.

My Dearest James, In these pages we can be
together. Let us meet here in the white spaces

between one word's ending and another's beginning.
Love Kate. December, 1907.

4. Books

The weight of books. Their bulk
and physical space; how they pull

downwards in the hand
like a plumb-line sighted at the ground.

The shape and texture of thought, folded
and folded again like the lung's tennis-court of flesh.

Mind's fingerprint and after image.
All that we're remembered by when we're finished.

The Horologist's Dream of Silence

A watch stripped of all embellishments
and the vanities of his craft. A masterwork.
Last night he dreamt of it again. In the strange

half-light of his workshop time breathes
in his hands. He leans down to it slowly
as though listening for the heartbeat of a child.

He hears an orchestra of whispers there: the spinning
wheel and spindle, the move and counter move
of the ratchet, the centrifuge of the hammer.

It is time made audible as music or a sound so pure
it is the closest he has come to silence. He listens.
All the lost voices of his childhood return

from the darkness, the crack of gunshot in the streets
at daybreak, the heavy boots climbing the staircase.
If he could only tell them he survived he might

redeem their sacrifice, make time whole again.
He rubs the sleep from his eyes – will go on trying.

Touch

This is the closest we come
to knowing each other
stumbling as we do with hands
outward to feel clumsily
for a face, a hand, a breast,
each other's touch.

And we forget the rest,
play each other like broken instruments
straining after a lost note –
our awkward, tender counterpoint.

*

I know you by touch the way
one body knows another
in the darkness, our hands

restless and exact
as they cross the distance
to find each other waiting

– our lost maps and slow
journey back to where we begin:
our chance origin.

*

At first light my hand
reaches out for you.

You have already left. Outside
the city wakes. I turn

into your absence and trace
an outline with my open palm,

feel a faint warmth still clinging
to the tossed covers like

a parting thought
and promise that we keep

in the cold light of day
to which we wake.

Burn

Not so much
a first memory
as a first scar,

my mother
burning sticks
in the yard.

An ember escapes
from the fire
glows in the dirt,

a marvellous
orange.
I reach down

pick it up
to the sudden
sickening burn

to my fingers
and thumb.
Tears, my hand

in a basin
of cold water
all afternoon.

Anniversary

We walk along the oak-lined paths
your tight-paced step soon leaving dad and me
behind to the mumble of our casual words.
We find you motionless by the boundary wall.

Twenty-five Novembers have now passed
and still each one you have mourned for her,
your damaged child too soon gone from you,
your daughter of twelve days of infant life.

Mother, I have wished with every breath
to restore her to you, strong and whole.
I who was born from those days of loss,
for the small child lying in the angel's plot.

1995

'Caitríona, had she lived…'

Caitríona, had she lived, would be forty now,
my near-twin, sister of the shadows,
understanding everything in her silence.
I wonder sometimes what life
she would've made, what home and husband
she might have found, the children
scrambling in the frantic kitchen
of the school-day morning, she marshalling
the chaos with a quiet insouciance.

But she's not here, there's no home or hearth
or children to visit, no serious husband
tinkering with the car in the garage.
I think of her instead in some imagined place,
spared the world-injury and damage
of those who go on, perfected by absence
into the confidante of my thoughts,
the counsellor of some private grief or doubt,
always listening but saying nothing.

I miss her the way I miss a face
I almost glimpsed, or the swallows that nested
in the garden that childhood summer, nurtured on crumbs,
until they left in the autumn and never returned,
the sky beyond the window grown dim.
Through such small runes I have tried to make her live.
Caitríona, sister I never had.

A Stone

An inert mass in the palm,
egg-like, smoothed by weather,
too cold to be living or dying.

The furious energies of matter
are arrested here, made still for a moment
like a breath held under water.

In the grain and speckles of its surface
is a chronicle in miniature
of sky and earth, a prehistory

of spirit; then letting go, the invisible
magic of release and fall,
gravity's angel in the undergrowth.

The Mathematician at Midnight

'This mysterious [π]… which comes in at every door and
window, and down every chimney'
— Augustus De Morgan, *A Budget of Paradoxes*

Receding into
the animal dark
that prowls at the edge
of the square
of white parchment:
the number.

Return
or never return
to the room
the breeze lifting
the curtains lightly
the sound of footfalls
echoing through the corridors
the remote
orderly arguments
straining for an audience.
The silence also.

Return.
Say nothing
let the secret slip
across the page
and disappear forever
into the margin.
Let someone else speak of it
and shake the world on its axis.

*

But it pulls him onwards
like an exotic insect
scuttling across the page
and descending into
the numbered dark.
Descending . . .

*

The number will not stop
turns in on itself
like a strange contraption
disgorging itself digit by digit
into ever smaller pieces
each horizon yet another version
of itself that can almost be grasped
but never reached.

His murmuring echoes against the stillness.
There is no end to it.
No end. The infinite and unknown
close around him like a shell
against the mind's self-imposed limits
and half-understood workings
its necessary genuflection
at the summit.

π is known as an irrational number. This means that it cannot be expressed as a fraction and the decimal expansion of such a number never repeats or terminates, unlike rational numbers. In ancient times the revelation of the nature of irrational numbers was considered to be an offense punishable on pain of death by drowning. Using computers π has been expanded to a trillion decimal places – and still counting.

Einstein's Compass

The boy's not right.
He sits in that room all day
mouth open like a fish,
tongue tied in his head.

When he speaks, he speaks
too slowly like that fool
Wolfgang in the butcher shop
stumbling over his words

while cutting your meat too small.
When the child looks at you
his eyes get closer together
as though he doesn't see you

but searches for something
that is beyond your shoulder.
His mind is with the birds.
He won't play with tin soldiers

like other boys his age,
but stands by the window
clutching that compass
his father gave him for Christmas.

It is a stopped clock,
the needle always pointing
north towards the spire
of St Mary's on the Hill.

When will the boy learn,
that it will never do otherwise,
that he breaks his mother's heart
with his silent vigils?

The Moons

All day he has waited for the light to fade
as carts and carriages rattled by in the courtyard
below his window, the shouts of traders
in the marketplace filling the air till dusk.

Now all has grown quiet in the narrow streets
as Orion climbs from the south and the cathedral bell
intones the solemn note of the Angelus over Padua.
He warms his hands by the dying embers of his fire,

then aims his telescope above the rooftops
of the merchants' houses on the square,
high above their world of commerce and trade,
their balanced ledgers and numbered hours.

And how, on looking closer, the sky explodes
in the viewfinder, the night more profligate
than he could've ever imagined it,
the Seven Sisters, shimmering and familiar,

rising above the horizon and Jupiter, brightest point
in all the darkness overhead, swims into focus
its four moons fixed in their circuits,
circling like ghostly presences across the shifting

weather of another planet. Such strange seasons
he has witnessed in the heavens but none like this
giant storm churning in the distance, its blooded iris
searching him out across the empty spaces

as though it were the eye of God that had found him
framed in this window, his failing sight
his only proof against all ignorance and doubt
that sometimes the heart can miss a beat

and is never quite the same after.

Dragonflies

This is dragonfly weather,
the air thick with pollen dust,
the canal bank an explosion of colour
as hedgerows come into blossom.

And then my eye catches them,
the minute flickers on the retina
of the metallic reds, greens and blues
of the dragonflies, the restless

shuttle of their flight-paths
as they dart from one point to another
plotting the water's surface
with their ghost geometries.

And then as I hunker down
at the water's edge, it is there:
the flame-red exclamation of a demoiselle
at eye level, its weightless flicker

and pulse as it hovers above
the surface, a vector of pure thought
poised and ready for movement
should I as much as quiver.

And I do quiver, stared out
there in the morning sunlight
by the glass-eyed crystalline glare
of the living, the air trembling

with a felt absence as the dragonfly
disappears into the shadows
like a faded apparition
of what had been made

knowable to the senses.

The Permanence of Stones

As a child
he placed
a fallen leaf
in his copybook
pressed down
hard
found a faint
impression
on the page
afterwards.

I A Crack in the Pavement

The knowledge of memory exists from the moment we begin to forget. Visiting his old family home he saw a crack in the pavement leading to the house. As a child it was a great canyon sneaking across the paving, the grass a distant savannah beyond it. He has never known a place so intimately since.

That crack in the pavement, a line through which a faint light seeps.

II Nostalgia

The desire that we all shared the same past. As a boy he stood in a field of corn and watched as a crow swooped down from the sky and almost touched his outstretched hand. In memory the field islanded, until there is only the afterthought of that moment with the crow, the idea of it. How when he has misplaced it, it will cease to exist.

The loneliness of forgetfulness.

III Where?

Where does the pain begin? If there was an archaeology of self, a stripping back strata by strata until you could find the root of your sorrow; but there is only the flawed cinema of memory, the stuttering image on the screen, a shadow play of hands against a wall. And all the things you needed most, cuttings on the floor, hiding the forgotten hurt that will not leave you alone.

IV Toy Soldier

He is like the tin soldier he loved as a child whose mechanism of cogs and springs had broken one day in summer. And so the toy became lifeless as the rain tapped out his loss against the windowpane. But it is more than being broken, those days when he cannot go on. He is not frozen in a stance, like the tin soldier, but must live through it in motion. It is the mind in chaos, a pushing and shoving in the darkness. It is, to him, as though the inner laws were at any moment to suddenly falter, as though atoms would cave in upon themselves, churches that have stood for centuries shake in their foundations and tumble.

As though, in each moment, the world continues on only by some accident.

V Loss

On days when he thinks he can't go on he is a tight-rope walker. The cable stretches out into the darkness, no sound echoing back from the distance. There is nothing to hold to but the slim wire of instinct, to put one foot in front of the other and move slowly out into the emptiness.

On days when he thinks he cannot go on, he does go on.

VI A Photograph

He sees a photograph of himself as a boy. He stands by a
chestnut tree dressed in scout's uniform, arms straight down
by his side. He does not smile, but seems kind, a wave of
thick, blonde hair creeping from beneath his cap. It is
strange to see himself marooned in time, his ghostly,
younger face just another in a gallery of lost faces that
crowd together in the mind – forgotten actors in a silent
scene.

VII The Permanence of Stones

The permanence of stones, their mass and bulk a presence,
their shape a containment, a place we can imagine but never
see. And the desire to go beyond the surface of things, to not
just see the world and its objects but *be* the world and its
objects, as sometimes he was in childhood.

The Rings

Washing my face my eye catches
the silver of the ring on my left hand.
The surprise, every time!

My face stares back at me from the mirror,
your naked body pale in the shadows
as you bend to recover your dress

from the floor. I turn.
There are such moments when we could
almost believe . . . such moments.

*

How last night in the hotel lobby the power
failed again and we gathered around the gaslight
with the others, Mohammed playing drums

and telling jokes I had already heard in Dublin,
the Americans and their stories of the desert.
How you said so little, while I, tempted at every turn,

elaborated on the details of our life together –
you, silent and unhappy in the shadows.
How one smile would've been enough.

*

That day in Dublin before we left,
the rain bucketed down on us.
We walked out among the city streets oblivious
in a trance of expectation.

Then stopping at a stall on College Green
bought two matching silver rings –
cover for our travelling together
in Islamic North Africa, our faked marriage

and imaginary honeymoon in better
weather. We laughed at the silliness of it,
but pressed the rings deep into our pockets
and thought of nothing else all evening.

*

Today I find your ring on the dresser.
Last night before you went to sleep
I noticed how, tired of unnecessary
fictions, you placed it there,
and I knew that you would not wear it again.

The Erg Chebbi

We had decamped to
a small hotel on the edge
of the sands, keeping
the same hours as the locals,
rising early and sleeping
all afternoon, the Erg Chebbi
a vast dune beyond our window
as we woke drowsy with heat
in the stifling bedroom.

I assumed, like you, that the desert
was a place without features,
the forms it took as temporary
as the seasons that shaped it,
but Ahmed told us over dinner
that the erg had marked the passage
of nomads for generations
until his grandfather abandoned
his itinerant life and built
a small clay house in its shadow.

So in the evening we set out
to climb that awesome sentinel,
the earth giving way beneath our feet
with each trudging step we took
upwards towards the stick figures
lined against the summit.
Reaching them finally,
we sat looking out from the brim,
an ocean of sand and wind
stretching out to the horizon,
the erg an eerie blood-red
in the low light of evening.

And it took our breaths away,
this alien landscape and its
hidden geography, this place
beyond borders into which
we had stumbled. It was
as beautiful and strange to me
as the craters of the moon
that rose above our heads
as you played like a child
with the sand at your feet –
and you were more lovely still,
my sweet.

Bella

'Her silences are my silences, her eyes, my eyes. It is as if Bella had
known me forever, as if she knew all my childhood, all my present,
all my future.'

– Ma Vie, Marc Chagall

Now that I'm too old to hold a brush,
I paint you again each morning with words:
Double Portrait With Wineglass,
Bella With Carnation, The Lover's Bouquet…

My mind is filled with colour still;
with each stroke you are there again, my bride,
lying on our crimson bed, our wedding night.
Things have changed. You wouldn't like it much.

The green violinist now grumbles
into his prayer book, has retired to an old
people's home in the suburb, refuses
to play me a tune on his purple fiddle.

Lovers no longer fly over fields or church spires,
milk cows in their Sunday best, go to the circus —
but still I keep them alive, the images.
I have been cursed, my love, with long life,

you dead now more than forty summers.
The old grandfather clock has finally stopped,
your absence no longer measured
by its metronome, the slow arm of loss.

I count the silent hours till I give up
the ghost. You stand before me,
again My Fiancée In Black Gloves.
My soul is vivid blue. It will know you.

Homecoming

'In the Gulags, there were no mirrors.'

– Anon

Once said to have been as beautiful
as Comrade Stalin's bride,
she has returned to her home in the village
to finds things much the same as before
but covered now by a veil
of neglect and dust.

And like a schoolgirl complimented
for her looks, she runs
to her old room to see
her face again in her grandmother's
gilded mirror above the bed:

she sees her mother's face
not her own, the fine features
blurred beyond recognition,
her nose broken, teeth rotten, raven hair
grey at the root.

And in the room she left
as a young woman, she chokes
to speak the altered syllables
of her name but cannot, wishes
every mirror in the world
smashed, blacked out,
banished forever.

Sky Burial

*The film stutters to a start as the camera searches
the bleached slope and comes into a brief focus:
barely visible against the white, two stick figures
climb the sheer ice-face of the col, move slowly
upwards into the cloud . . .*

The eerie spectacle of death postponed:
your bare shoulders protruding
from the snow like an exhumed mummy's,

your fingers still clutching the mountainside
as though you would crawl on hands and knees
to the summit you never reached.

The dumbstruck climbers gather round.
In your pocket an unpaid bill for gloves, rope,
a letter from your wife with news of home.

The cracked altimeter and maps in your bag
give no clues to those final hours lost
on the slope as snow-blind you stumbled

in the dark, tripped to your death.
It's too high here even for the birds to scavenge
and return you piece by piece to the heavens,

so the climbers endure the cold for another hour,
perform their own sky burial of sorts
and make a human grave of piled stones

on the mountainside. They pull close,
say a final prayer before the light goes down,
then begin their slow descent

to the base-camp below.

Offerings

A woman in a blue
swimsuit swims out
into the blue sea
as a bank of rain-cloud
drifts in from the islands.
Out by the pier
the swans in groups
huddle by the harbour wall
float on stillness.
Beyond the horizon
the ceaseless swell
and fall as the ocean's
slow muscle flexes
the waves stealing
another inch as
the tide creeps in leaving
bottles and shells
on the beach
small offerings of debris
to an indifferent day.

A Stone Witness

Eye that never blinks,
that has watched the sun
rise above the waves a million times,
then disappear again;
that has seen the flare
of a comet among the stars,
the death of stars.

Eye that watched as strange red sails
gathered on the horizon
to the sound of thunder and musket,
the bloated bodies of soldiers
that washed up on the beach
for weeks afterwards.

Eye that never tires
of looking,
that watched as a teenage girl
waded into the freezing surf,
released a white parcel
into the water, wept
as it floated out into the darkness.

Eye that has seen rain fall
like tears of longing, the sun
burn like a promise.
Eye that sees nothing —
                    will go on looking.

Rock Ammonite

The surprising simplicity of it
there among the shoal:
little earth-memory,
spiralling palimpsest.

It is the alpha and omega
of necessity, the first word
and the last of all
argument. And if the eye

is steady retrace the slow
turning of centuries
and descend step-wise,
down the tight curve

of its spine to the centre
about which all appears
to turn. And there,
close your eyes

and push one step further,
past language and origins
into the dark beginnings
of it all.

On Broken Hill

My bones the bare evidence
of remote life,
named after this place
which was once nameless.

And no trace there
in the starched bones
of the precise weight of memory,
experience, loss;

of those final moments
on the hillside watching
the antelope by the water's edge
with eyes that you would recognise

as your own as the red sun
dropped out of the red sky.
I had neither the strength
nor desire to take life,

my darkened brain ablaze
with as many points of fire
as the river of stars
emerging overhead.

The Lost Word

The way a word can bring everything back
but itself. You tell me of summer. A room. Him
sitting by the window fixed on a book,
you searching the dictionary
for a word he doesn't know:
That which was once thought to be true
and is now found to be false.
Then crossing that room,
you whispered the word into his ear, over
and over, as sharp on the tongue
as the word *desire*.

The way that word, now lost,
empties our conversation of all words in
this high-ceilinged café, teases
your brain into a corner
where I can no longer reach you
(a cave, say, where words are palpable as stones
but silent).

I watch as our coffees grow cold on the red tabletop
and you puncture the silence with wild guesses –
axis, no not axis, sounds like… crisis…
Then as you put on your scarf and black
winter coat it comes back, forms itself
on your lips without fuss: *Ersatz!*

Ersatz. I force a smile at your discovery
too embarrassed to mention that
I've never heard the word before this moment,
wait as you write it on your hand, then mine,
so we will never forget it:
A poor substitute,
one who could never replace another.

Autumn

Outside the window, the junk
of the day falling on pavements,
the toaster humming to nothing.

Baltic Amber

Suspended in a bead of amber the ant
dreams itself to perfection, caught
as the bark bled its juices and the resin hardened
in the afternoon heat of the Palaeolithic.
And so it is frozen there, its antennae
raised in some final gesture
of fright and sacrifice, its tiny insect eyes
magnified and looking out to where
I face it on the page: emblem and lifeline
of all that perishes, all that survives.

Talking in Whispers

In memory of Bernard O'Brien

I

We drive in my father's car,
the morning drizzle streaking across the windshield
as the wipers beat a mantra against the day.
It is cold. We do not talk.
Your pain, Bernard, felt there on the empty roads.

II

Larger than life. Chancer. Mischief-maker.
Wild in the way my mother was sober,
arm wrestling my older brothers at the kitchen table
after finishing your milk-round in the lorry,
driving the back roads from Finglas
and dropping in for tea on the way home.

There was the time you were nearly killed.
Parked in a farmer's lane at dusk,
your truck rolled back on you as the handbrake slipped –
you were pinned down between a hedge
and a concrete wall under five tons of milk,
the tangle of branches softening your landing.

Miracle man, you walked away unhurt,
defying the odds. Arm in a sling you laughed it off
in the hallway drinking tea with my mam.
A truck for heaven's sake! she finally relented,
her favourite brother saved from himself again.
You seemed indestructible in the driveway as you left.

Maybe you were just lucky.

III

'He is talking in whispers,' my father says at last,
'the way your aunt Debbie talked before she died,
so quiet you could hardly hear her

whispering into the darkness of the room…
All the family leaning close in those final hours
until she could no longer feel us there by her bedside.

The first of my sisters to make the journey.'

IV

All week the signs are bad. You tease and pick
at your food but cannot eat. The soup
and milk they give you lie untouched
on the tray. The doctors dodder.
The platelets in your blood count
rise and fall from one hour to another,
your body struggling against the *chemo*
and its endless chemical bombardment,
your only comfort in the unbearable minutes,
the slow oblivion of the pain-killer injection
working its way into your system.

V

It was to be a fresh start. At fifty-six
you were packing it in after years with the dairy,
buying a taxi plate and a new *Mondeo*.
A cushy number, you said to my father.
Make your own hours.
No one to answer to in the morning.
Drive and talk. Talk and drive.
What could be easier after thirty years
behind the wheel of an articulated lorry
once you had a good map and a flask of coffee
to guide you through the endless traffic
and the cross-hatched maze of housing estates
that stretch from Blanchardstown to Tallaght.

You were anxious though behind the bravura,
starting over now that the kids were married.
Your new life at mid-life
an unmarked road ahead of you into the morning sunlight.

VI

Yesterday dad told me that mam cried
in the hospital corridor after she had visited you.
Shocked at how you looked, hollowed out, grey, frightened,
finally seeing what she had denied for weeks.
That you are maybe dying there in the Mater Hospital
with all the other terminal cases.

Maybe. Today she clutches to her rosary
and passes the beads through her fingers
like knucklebones, counting the hours,
the days, the weeks, the thoughts that you have left,
whispering her prayers to the silence of the kitchen
as though God would listen to those
who speak almost inaudibly of their sorrow.

VII

But you make it back somehow from the brink,
your blood-cells pounded with the *chemo* making the fight
that we all hope we will never have to face,

the cancer retreating from your ravaged body
like a flood subsiding after a terrible downpour
leaving a flattened landscape in its wake.

For now at least. Who knows the future?
We talk in whispers and say it over.
Inhale. Exhale. Heal. Return to the living.

Take all you can in this morning of remission.

His Hands

I loved to watch his hands
while he worked, the way
he prepared the surface first

with a wipe of his cloth,
then softened his brushes
in turpentine, the sharp smell

filling my lungs in the shed.
He would chalk an old string,
ask me to hold one end

as he plucked on it to make a line,
and again and again until he had
a grid of lines like

a page of sheet music without the notes,
or my old school copybook
waiting for words.

And with the short
rough strokes of his pencil
the outline of the letters would form

on the polished grain:
Bell & Swastika: Dublin's
Finest Laundry, est. 1910.

He would mix the paint
on his palette, apply the large
ox-hair brush for sweeps of colour,

his hand's careful rhythm
as he made the curve of an *s*,
the straight back of an *f*.

And then as the evening pressed
against the glass, he'd take
the narrow hair-line sable

from its case, test its tiny tip
with thumb and forefinger
then steady his hand above each letter

as he made the precise,
delicate strokes needed
to make the letter edge perfect.

Afterwards, in the darkening light
he would knead the colours
from each brush in turn,

oblivious then, or so it seemed,
to the plastic and *stick-on* shop-front craze
that spelt in stark outline

the fate of his dying trade,
of his hand's patient work
and the casual rituals of his craft

that I did not fully understand
back then but reach for now
as I test the line and contour

of my hand and find
my father's touch in mine,
filling the unmarked page with words

as night comes on.

Your Photographs

Those days in late spring and early summer
when you would come to life again
after the dark months of autumn and winter,
like the flowers you so loved to find
out there in the woods past Reilly's Farm:
the chance constellations of Bloodroot and Shooting Stars,
Foxglove, Sundew, Oconee Bells.

I had my mug of strong coffee and morning paper,
and my work to keep me busy while you were away
    till evening
out there in the world with your old Nikon camera,
'Chasing the present moment like a Sufi,' you quipped
as you gathered your things in the hallway
before you left. And then as you turned in the door:
'To forget it when it's gone.'

Still, you kept those pictures you so carefully composed,
catalogued each print with the studied diligence
of a museum curator poring over the treasures of the past:
your snapshot photographs, too avant-garde
for the neighbours to admire, the blossoms adrift
in a haze of blues, yellows, reds,
as you spent the evenings locked away in your attic
    dark-room,
lost among ghost-flower negatives
hanging on pegs or dipped in basins of chemicals.

I still keep those photographs in an old black box
with all the other keepsakes and bric-a-brac
that I hadn't the heart to make a funeral pyre with after
     you left.
I pore over them now in the home we so briefly shared
trawling the memoried dark for all the signs I missed
in the slow unmaking of our happiness.

'To forget it when it's gone,' you said.
Forget it when it's gone.

The Silence After

'The honeybee is often described as a domesticated insect. This is
wholly inaccurate. The honeybee is a wild bee. Man has never
succeeded in domesticating it in the way he has domesticated other
animals.'
— *The World of Ants, Bees & Wasps*, Brian Vesey-Fitzgerald

He stayed in his study all morning,
and when I went to him
he was standing by the window, his face
turned towards the garden
and the distant droning of the hive.

Do you notice how the note
has changed, he said, *how it grows*
lower and more certain? The bees
are about to swarm. They will gorge
themselves on honey, then be gone.

It is a beautiful sight and every
beekeeper's shame: the bees spilling
from the hive at noon, the Queen
in flight among them; the cacophony
of wings, the silence after.

I should meet them at the hive's
entrance as they leave, make my loud
lamentation with pot and spoon, try
coax the Queen back to her throne ...
This time, I will let them go.

After the bees had flown, he walked
in the garden among his flowers;
his fingers stained a pollen-brown
from lilac, rose, sweet-meadow,
when he returned to the house at dusk.

He was silent then as he stood among
the white frames of the bee boxes
in the hall, as though his thoughts had fled
with the swarm, his heart as empty as the hive
he could not bring himself to look at anymore.

Passage

I make my passage across the city, the bus idling
in morning traffic, I idling with my thoughts
and sorrow. This the first anniversary of your going.

There, finally, beneath the breaking clouds I stand among
the granite headstones, the tattered flags
and votive toys, the faded plastic flowers.

On every grave there is a snapshot of the departed
cut from some family scene and smiling towards us
in the blue, pristine sky of their absence.

All those lost faces and you among them,
on a hill where no tree grows and the wind blows cold.
We must all rest somewhere. You were my father.

I loved you imperfectly, but true.
To the deep, dark earth we have given you.

Swallows

'During the Old Kingdom, swallows were associated with stars
and therefore the souls of the dead. Chapter 86 of the *Book of the
Dead* specifically instructs the deceased on how to transform into a
swallow.'

– Egyptian Myth

The day after I wrote your poem
the swallows came, flashing by
my window in the smoky light of evening,
their new nest the eave above my bedroom.

It was as if you had offered
a reply to my question, a sign to one
who had lost faith in such meanings,
these creatures who have navigated north

for millennia arriving at my door
when I least expected them.
They have plotted a course through
my hesitant brain as though

in each sweeping trajectory of flight
I have heard, finally, your voice.

Notes

p. 16 *The Beekeeper to his Assistant*
'...like Einstein's vision...' In 1905 Einstein proposed that light had a particle nature, also referred to as photons or light quanta.

p. 25 *Fossil*
'Ambulacra'. The five radial areas on the undersurface of the starfish and similar echinoderms, from which the tube feet are protruded and withdrawn.

p. 42 *Einstein's Compass*
Einstein attributed his fascination with the laws of physics to the unwavering behaviour of the compass needle on the compass his father gave him as a child.

p. 43 *The Moons*
Galileo discovered the moons of Jupiter on 10th January 1610.

p. 54 *Sky Burial*
George Mallory and Andrew Irvine attempted the Everest summit on 8th June 1924. George Mallory's remains were found in June 1999 by Eric Simonson and a BBC documentary team.

p. 58 *On Broken Hill*
Broken Hill in Kabwe, Zambia, is the site of the discovered remains of an archaic *Homo Sapiens* male, dating from about 120,000 years ago.

About the Author

Noel Duffy was born in Dublin in 1971 and studied Experimental Physics at Trinity College, Dublin, before turning his hand to writing. He co-edited (with Theo Dorgan) *Watching the River Flow: A Century in Irish Poetry* (Poetry Ireland, 1999) and was the winner in 2003 of the START Chapbook Prize for Poetry for his collection, *The Silence After*. His work has appeared widely in Ireland (including *Poetry Ireland Review, Force 10* and *The Dublin Review*) as well as in the UK, the US, Belgium and South Africa.

More recently he was the winner of the *Firewords Poetry Award* and has been a recipient of an Arts Council of Ireland Bursary for Literature. A play, *The Rainstorm,* was produced for the Dublin Fringe Festival in 2006.

Noel holds an MA in Writing from the National University of Ireland, Galway, and has taught creative writing there as well as at the Irish Writers' Centre, Dublin, and scriptwriting at the Dublin Business School, Film Department. He currently lives in Dublin.